Made in the USA
Monee, IL
12 March 2022

92762909R10062